The Great Ecosystem Adventure
A Reference Book for Kids
Book 1

My website: www.weleduca.com

ISBN: 9798840686799

Preface...

My son inspired me to write this book. His repeated questions about ecosystems and environmental challenges sparked my curiosity, and I set out to learn more on my own about these topics. I thought it would be fun to take other children on the amazing learning adventure that my son and I have been having about ecosystems and collect my research findings in a book to benefit other children.

An ecosystem can be as small as an organism or as big as our world. Ecosystems provide for both diversity and creativity. Birds and bees get nectar from flowers, squirrels devour berries, and all of these animals are part of the same energy network. They all depend on each other for their own life.

Even when we are not aware of it, our existence as a component of an ecosystem has an influence on every element of our lives, whether consciously or unconsciously. Our environmental problems are mostly caused by a lack of understanding of our role in the world.

It is my belief that educating our children about ecosystems and the environment will impart valuable lessons that they will carry with them for life. The preservation of our planet and its wildlife can only be achieved if children are taught from an early age to respect and care for the natural world and its inhabitants.

Enjoy your learning journey!

Widad ELHANAFI

TABLE OF CONTENTS
An introduction to ecosystems for Kids

INTRODUCTION TO ECOSYSTEMS

What Does Ecosystem Mean?

Ecosystems are responsible for the diversity of life on our planet. Plant communities and animal communities are groups of organisms that coexist in an environment in order to sustain the survival of one another's existence. They include both plants and animals.

An ecosystem is a population of creatures that interact with one another and with their surroundings. Living things interact with one another as well as with non-living objects such as soil, water, and air, among other things. Ecosystems can be as tiny as your backyard or as huge as the ocean, and they frequently contain a great number of living organisms.

All living things are found in ecosystems. These ecosystems can be categorized and broken up into smaller ecosystems known as biomes, or biological zones, such as tropical rainforests or deserts. These zones have certain types of animals and plant life that are used to classify different types of ecosystems.

Where Do Ecosystems Come From?

FROM NATURE

Natural ecosystems are all around us! Existing long before you were born, nature has a way of collecting different species in one area.

FROM HUMANS

Artificial ecosystems are human-created systems with different varieties of plants, animals, and people living together in specific areas or regions.

Types of Ecosystems

Aquatic ecosystem

Terrestrial ecosystem

Ecosystems may be divided into two categories: **terrestrial** and **aquatic** ecosystems. Ecosystems situated on land are known as terrestrial ecosystems, whilst aquatic ecosystems may be found in bodies of water. It is possible to classify ecosystems more explicitly depending on the types of animals and plants that are interacting within the ecosystem, in addition to characteristics such as climate and other environmental conditions.

Aquatic Ecosystems

MARINE (SALT) WATER

You can find **marine water aquatic ecosystems** in a lot of places such as oceans, which make up 70% of the Earth's surface!!

FRESH WATER

Places with non-salty water are part of **fresh water aquatic ecosystems** (and no, swimming pools, puddles, and bathtubs don't count!).

WHAT YOU CAN FIND IN NATURAL AQUATIC ECOSYSTEMS

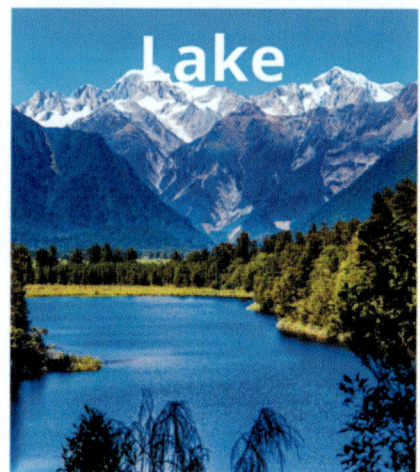

Sea

Sand

Ocean

Swamp

Waterfall

Lake

River

Seaweed

Pond

Terrestrial Ecosystems

TAIGA
Taiga biomes have tall trees like spruce and pine in cold climates.

TUNDRA
Tundra biomes are just as cold as the icy taiga, but without tall forests.

DECIDUOUS FORESTS
Deciduous forests' trees have leaves that they lose every fall.

GRASSLANDS
Grassland biomes have abundant grass, flowers, and herbs.

TROPICAL FORESTS
Tropical forests are hot, humid, and have diverse plant and animal life.

DESERTS
Desert biomes are hot and dry with sand, and have sparse plant life.

WHAT YOU CAN FIND
IN NATURAL TERRESTRIAL ECOSYSTEMS?

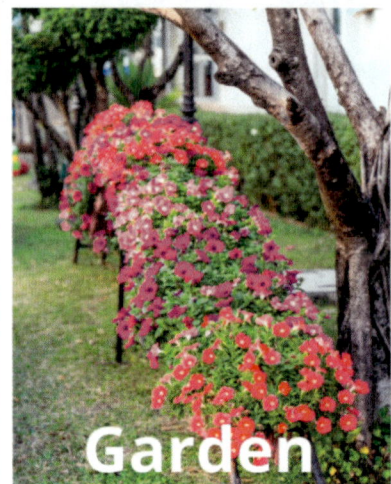

Trees

Rocks

Forest

Grass

Savannah

Garden

Polar Bears

Jungle

Ice

Mountains

Farm

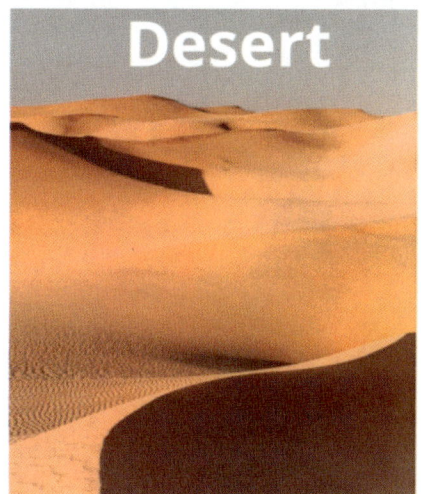

Desert

Artificial Ecosystems

Zoos and aquariums frequently build artificial ecosystems by relocating animals into human-made environments that are comparable to their natural habitat.

Aquarium

Zoo

Crop Field

Garden

The Food Chain

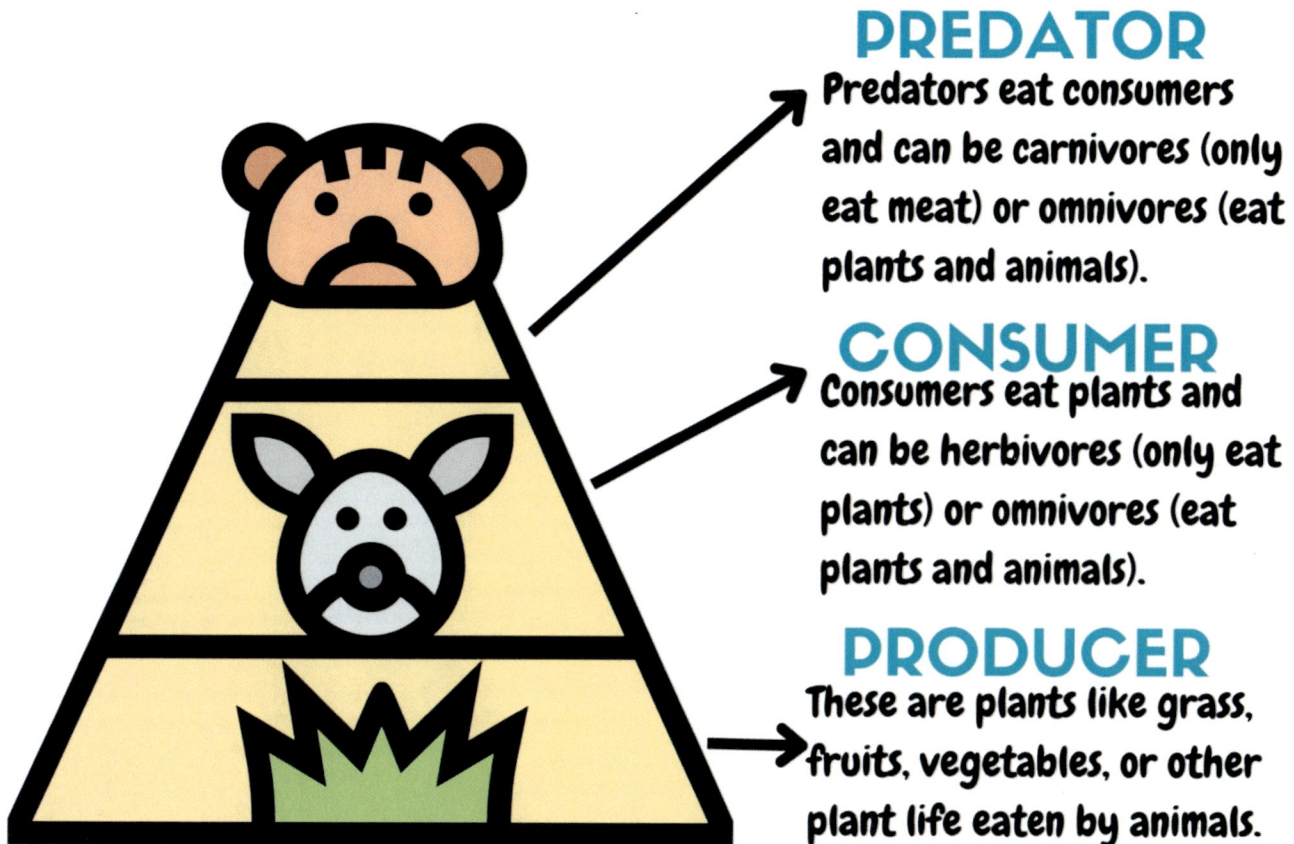

PREDATOR
Predators eat consumers and can be carnivores (only eat meat) or omnivores (eat plants and animals).

CONSUMER
Consumers eat plants and can be herbivores (only eat plants) or omnivores (eat plants and animals).

PRODUCER
These are plants like grass, fruits, vegetables, or other plant life eaten by animals.

Each food chain generally has three layers - predator, consumer, producer - with one or two connections for each layer. As animals consume their food, you can see a flow of energy up the pyramid to the very top. There can be some predators that are higher up in a food chain based on their speed, power, or food preferences compared to other animals in that ecosystem. A decomposer returns the remains of animals higher up in the food chain into nutrients for growing more producers.

THE FOOD CHAIN IS A CYCLE

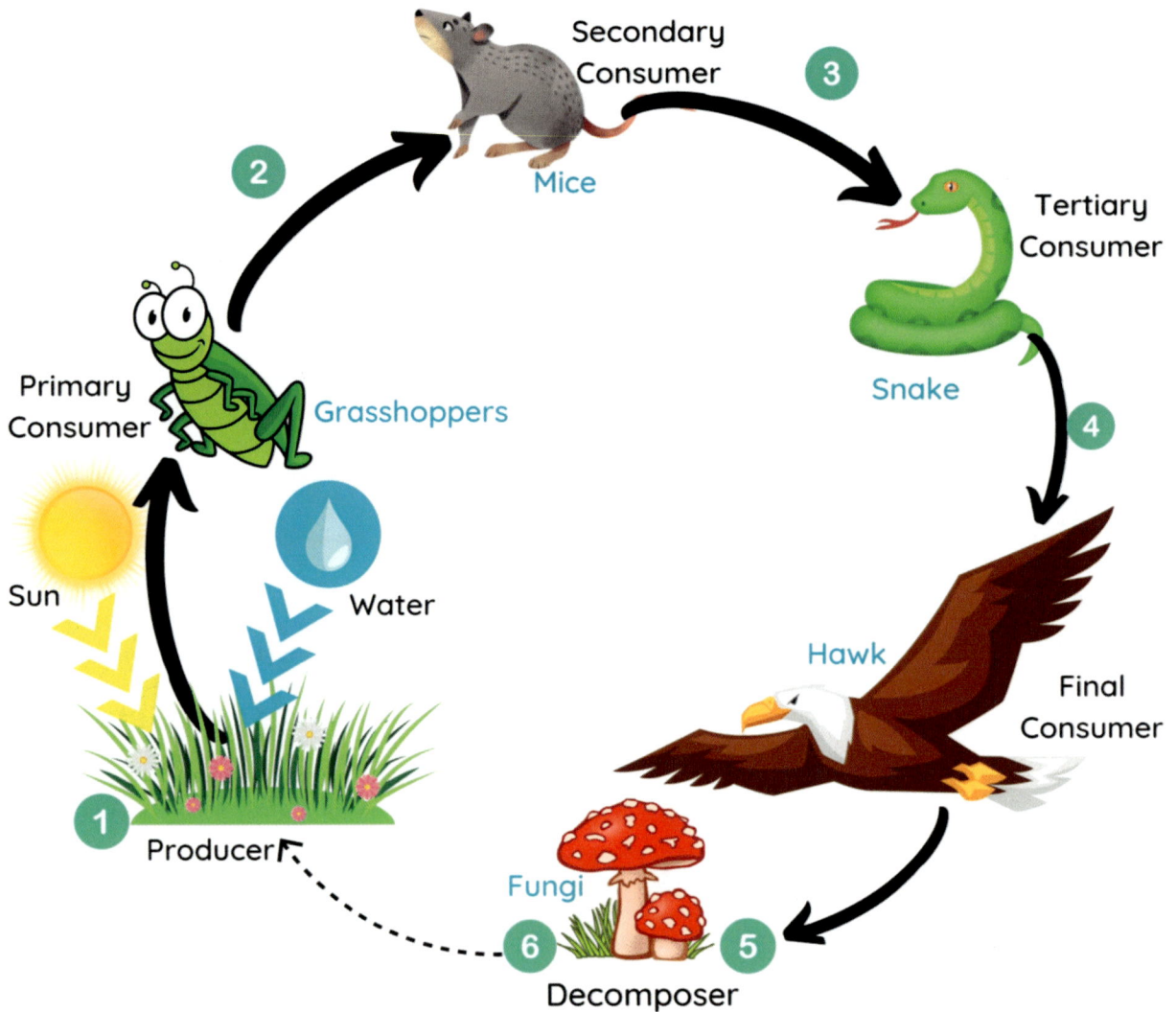

Secondary Consumer

Mice

Tertiary Consumer

Snake

Primary Consumer

Grasshoppers

Sun

Water

Hawk

Final Consumer

Producer

Fungi

Decomposer

1. Grass and plants eaten by grasshoppers.

2. The grasshoppers are eaten by the mice.

3. Mice are eaten by snakes.

4. The snakes are eaten by eagles.

5. Fungi decompose the dead hawks' corpses, turning them into nutrition.

6. Grass grows as a result of sunlight, water, and nutrients.

Food Chain VS Food Web

A food chain has one predator, one consumer, and one organism for each role!

FOOD CHAIN

A food chain is a simplified representation of the energy flow between organisms in an ecosystem.

FOOD WEB

A food web is a representation of the interactions that occur between the various food chains that make up an ecosystem.

A food web can have a lot of predators and organisms from other layers of the food chain!

Levels of organization: Part 1

1

Organism

Individual living thing.

A group of **organisms** of one species living in the same area.

Population

2

Community

3

Populations that live together in a defined area.

Levels of organization: Part 2
Organizing living things in their environments

4

Ecosystem

Community and its non-living environments (deer, hawk, elephant, snake, bison, grass, trees, air, etc.)

5

Biosphere

The part of Earth that contains all ecosystems

Individual

Population

Community

Ecosystem

Biome

LEVELS OF ORGANIZATION: PART 2 CONTINUED

Biosphere

The biosphere encompasses all of Earth's biomes and is the greatest level of biological organization. In addition to all living organisms on the planet, it contains nonliving factors that affect it, such as sunshine and water.

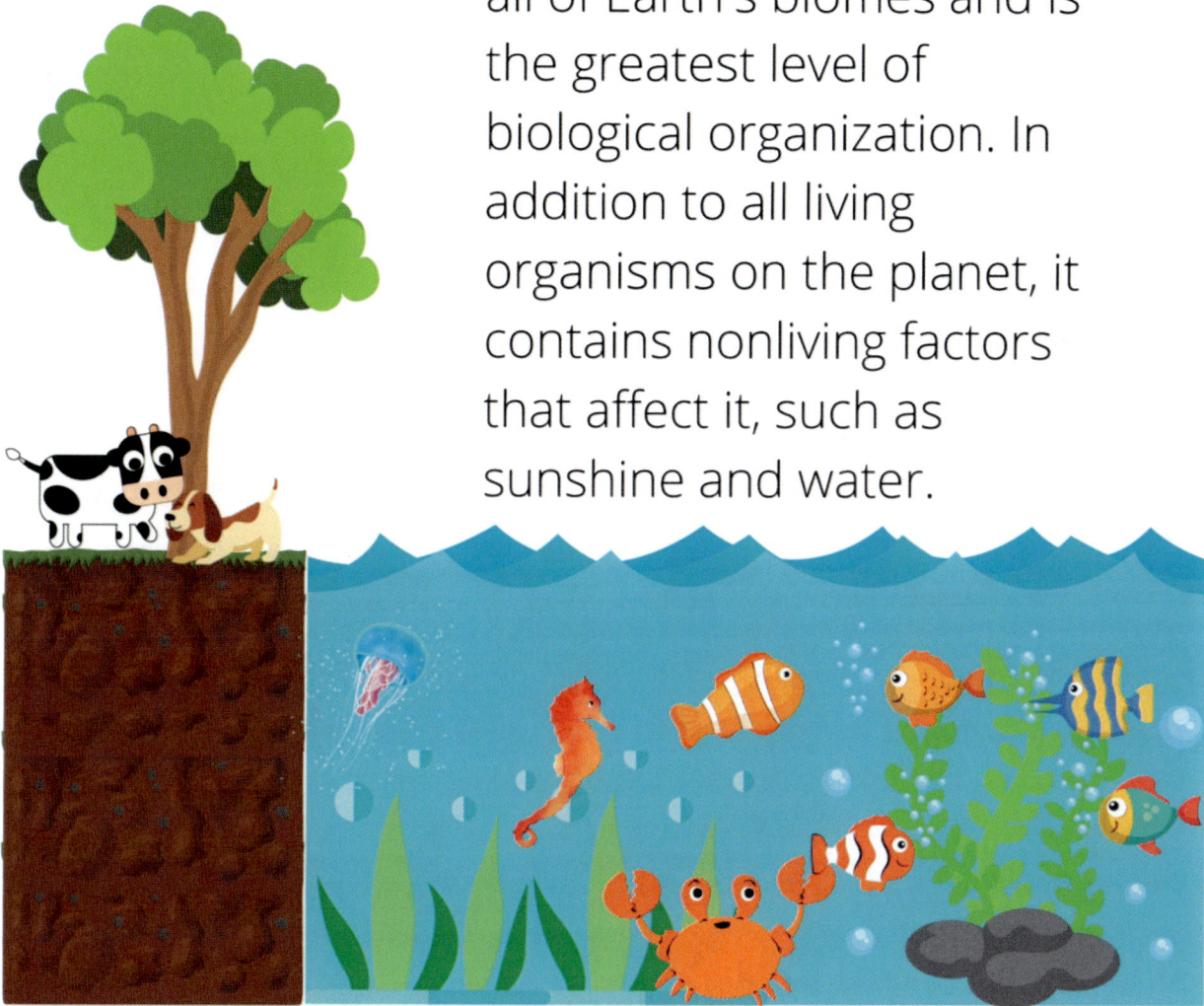

Biosphere: How is it different from a biome?

The Biosphere is made up of a variety of distinct biomes. A biome is a collection of ecosystems that belong to a certain region, whereas a biosphere is a collection of all biomes.

CONCLUSION

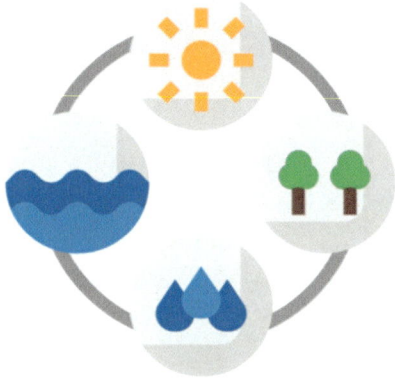

An ecosystem is a system of living organisms and their environment. The word comes from the Greek words for household (oikos) and system (sune).

Ecosystems can be found anywhere from the deep sea to a puddle on the ground. They can be large, like a forest, or small, like a pond. An ecosystem might be a place where you can find food, water, and shelter.

It might also be a place where you can learn about the different types of plants and animals.

21

Ecosystems come from a variety of places, including the sun, the air, the water, and the earth.

And as you have learned from this book, there are many different types of ecosystems, including aquatic, terrestrial, and artificial.

Practice and have fun

Now, it is time for you to put your knowledge into practice, and you can use the worksheets for that.

Worksheet 1-Levels of organization

In order to demonstrate a hierarchy of organizational levels and correspond with the correct image, rewrite each word and put it in the correct sequence on paper.

laudividni

ytinummco

puopnoital

metsysoce

erehposib

WORKSHEET 2- THE CYCLE OF THE FOOD CHAIN

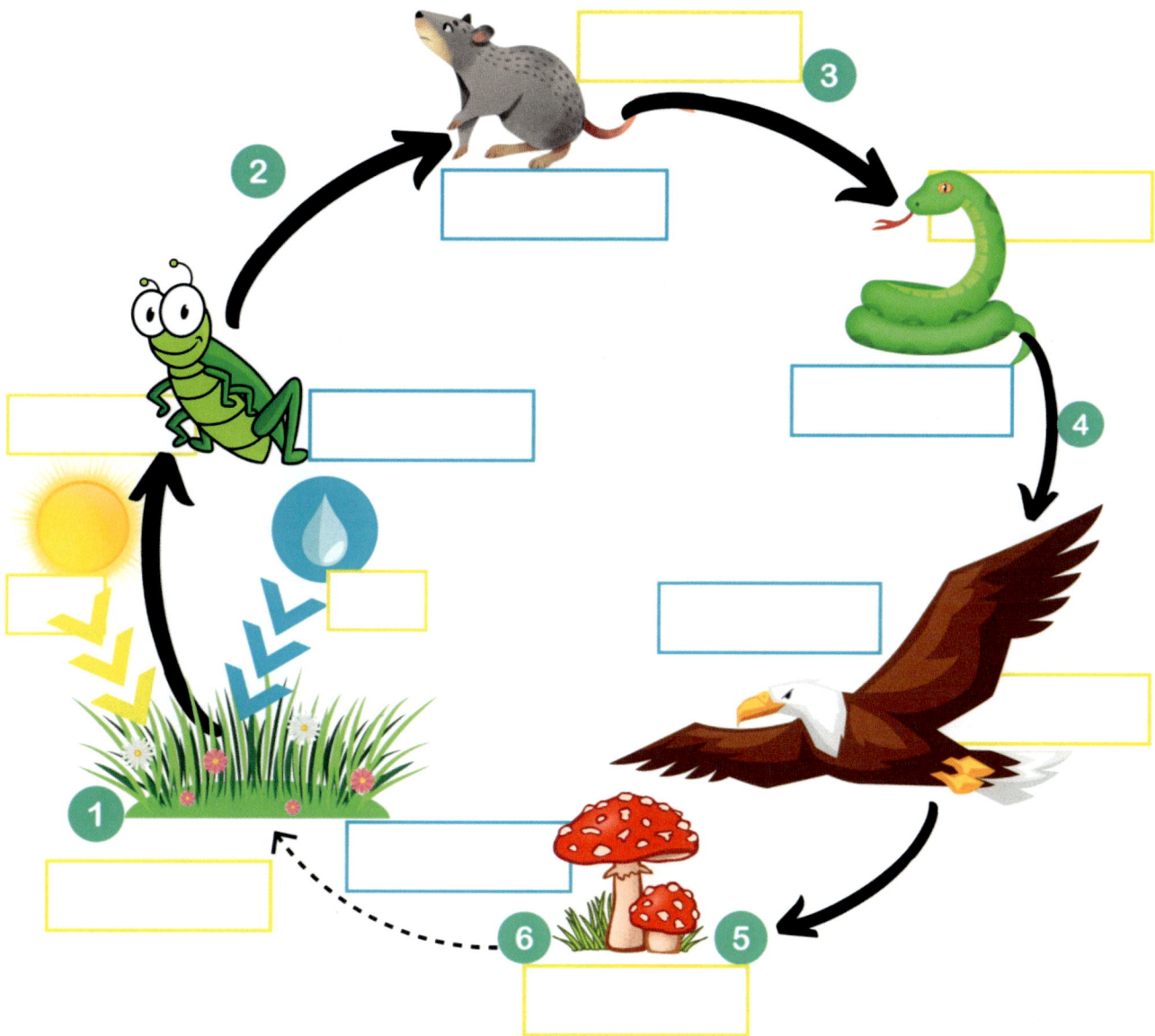

Complete the cycle with each food chain role with the right word:

Secondary Consumer   Decomposer   Final Consumer   Sun
Producer   Primary Consumer   Tertiary Consumer   Water

Complete with right name:

Snake   Grasshoppers   Fungi   Hawk   Mice

Worksheet 3–LEVEL OF ORGANIZATION
Match the column with correct pictures.

ECOSYSTEM

POPULATION

BIOSPHERE

INDIVIDUAL

ECOSYSTEM

Worksheet 4–TYPES OF ECOSYSTEM

Complete each sentence with the right word

AN ARTIFICIAL ECOSYSTEM	AQUATIC ECOSYSTEMS
TERRESTRIAL ECOSYSTEM	NATURAL ECOSYSTEM

.... occur naturally where organisms freely interact with other components. For example, forests mountains and grasslands etc.

.... is a human-made system of plants, animals and people living in an area together. For example, zoo parks and farms etc.

.... are ecosystems found only on land. For example, forests, deserts and grassland ecosystems etc.

.... are ecosystems found in bodies of water. For example, rivers, ponds, lakes and wetlands etc.

Worksheet 5- Levels of organization

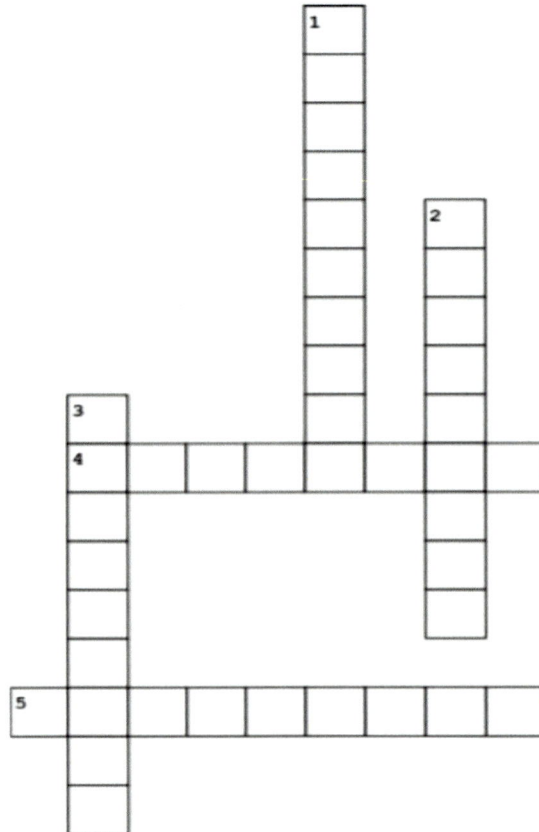

Down

1. A group of organisms of one species living in the same area.
2. Community and its non-living environments.
3. Populations that live together in a defined area.

Across

4. Individual living thing.
5. It encompasses all of Earth's biomes and is the greatest level of biological organization.

MY VOCABULARY

Use this sheet to note down all new words you learned in this book. Add a definition for each term. You can use a dictionary.

ECOSYSTEM

MY VOCABULARY

Use this sheet to note down all new words you learned in this book. Add a definition for each term. You can use a dictionary.

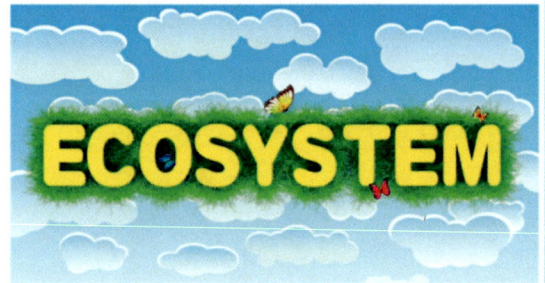

ECOSYSTEM

MY VOCABULARY

Use this sheet to note down all new words you learned in this book. Add a definition for each term. You can use a dictionary.

ECOSYSTEM

Made in the USA
Coppell, TX
02 March 2024